ENGINEERED BY NATURE

GIANT'S CAUSEWAY

BY MARTHA LONDON

CONTENT CONSULTANT
CHARLES E. JONES
SENIOR LECTURER
GEOLOGY AND ENVIRONMENTAL SCIENCES
UNIVERSITY OF PITTSBURGH

Kids Core
An Imprint of Abdo Publishing
abdobooks.com

abdobooks.com

Published by Abdo Publishing, a division of ABDO, PO Box 398166, Minneapolis, Minnesota 55439. Copyright © 2021 by Abdo Consulting Group, Inc. International copyrights reserved in all countries. No part of this book may be reproduced in any form without written permission from the publisher. Kids Core™ is a trademark and logo of Abdo Publishing.

Printed in the United States of America, North Mankato, Minnesota
042020
092020

Cover Photo: Ben Edek/iStockphoto
Interior Photo: Lucky Team Studio/Shutterstock Images, 4–5; Joe Gough/iStockphoto, 6; Serg Zastavkin/Shutterstock Images, 8; Red Line Editorial, 9 (pillar), 28–29; iStockphoto, 9 (basketball hoop), 17, 18, 28; Stefan Alfonso/iStockphoto, 9 (giraffe); Historica Graphica Collection/Heritage Images/Hulton Archive/Getty Images, 11; Lyd Photography/Shutterstock Images, 12; Ralf Lehmann/Shutterstock Images, 14–15; Shutterstock Images, 20–21; Sandra Mori/Shutterstock Images, 22; Ryan W. Curley Photography/Shutterstock Images, 25; James Griffiths Photography/iStockphoto, 26

Editor: Marie Pearson
Series Designer: Megan Ellis

Library of Congress Control Number: 2019954241

Publisher's Cataloging-in-Publication Data

Names: London, Martha, author.
Title: Giant's Causeway / by Martha London
Description: Minneapolis, Minnesota : Abdo Publishing, 2021 | Series: Engineered by nature | Includes online resources and index.
Identifiers: ISBN 9781532192852 (lib. bdg.) | ISBN 9781098210755 (ebook)
Subjects: LCSH: Giant's Causeway (Northern Ireland)--Juvenile literature. | Natural monuments--Juvenile literature. | Volcanic geology--Juvenile literature. | National parks and reserves--Juvenile literature. | Landforms--Juvenile literature.
Classification: DDC 910.202--dc23

CONTENTS

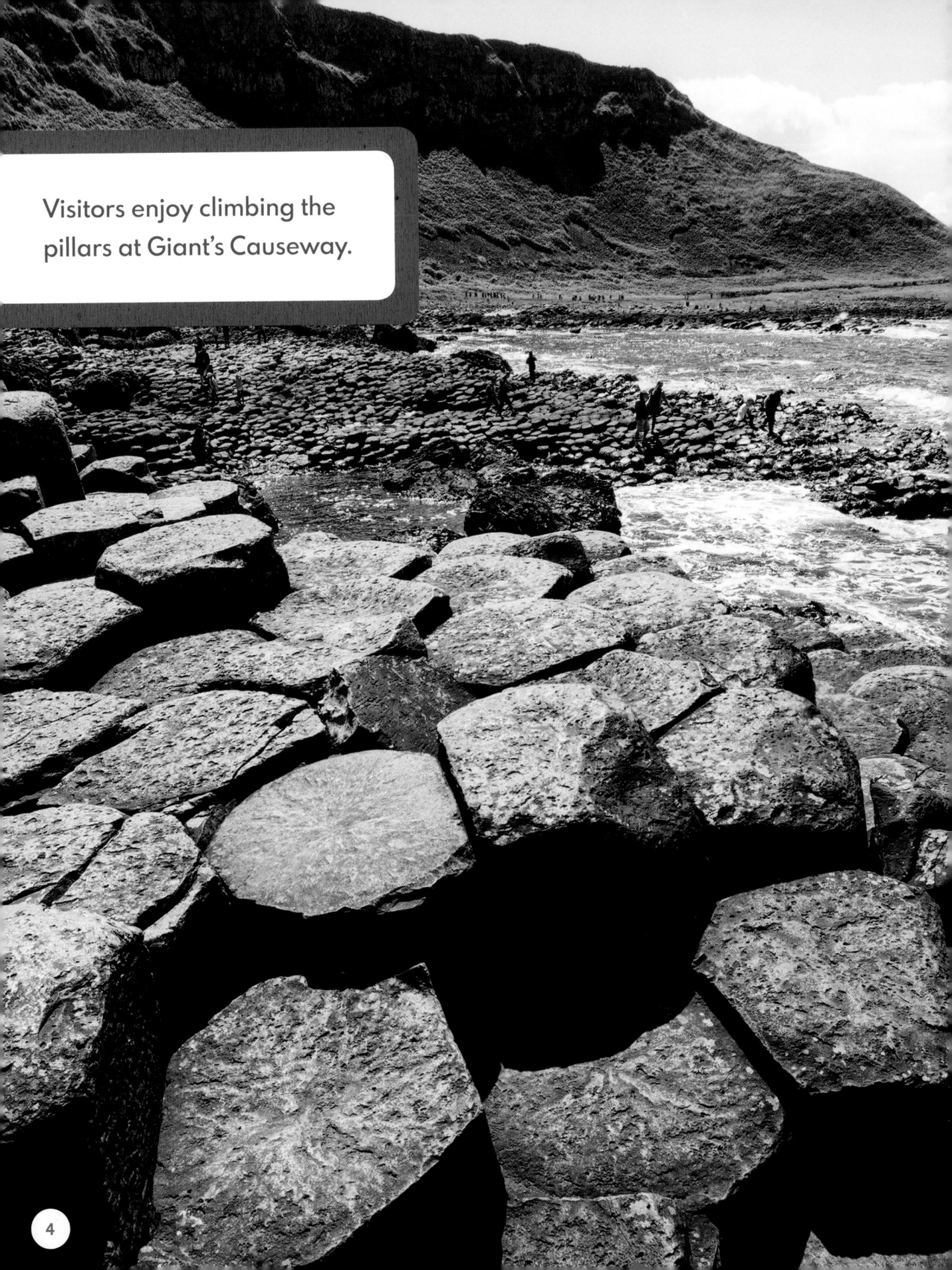

Visitors enjoy climbing the pillars at Giant's Causeway.

CHAPTER 1

FORMED BY GIANTS

A family hikes across Giant's **Causeway**. The rock pillars form a path for them. The kids leap from rock to rock. Around them, other visitors pose for pictures. Behind them, ocean waves crash on the beach.

Cliffs rise up behind the pillars.

The family moves away from the water and toward a hill. There, people look out over the causeway at the gray, black, and reddish pillars that line the shore. The family makes its way up the hill. The path climbs and climbs. Grass grows on the top of the cliff. From this angle, the great columns look as if they are holding up the cliff.

Giant's Organ

There are many large columns at Giant's Causeway. One of the largest collections of tall columns is the Organ. The columns line up next to one another. Each is approximately 39 feet (12 m) tall. The structure looks similar to organ pipes.

The Organ is one of the pillar formations at Giant's Causeway.

Building a Bridge

Giant's Causeway is in Northern Ireland. The area is located along the coast. It covers 4 miles (6 km) of coastline. Giant's Causeway

How Tall Is 39 Feet?

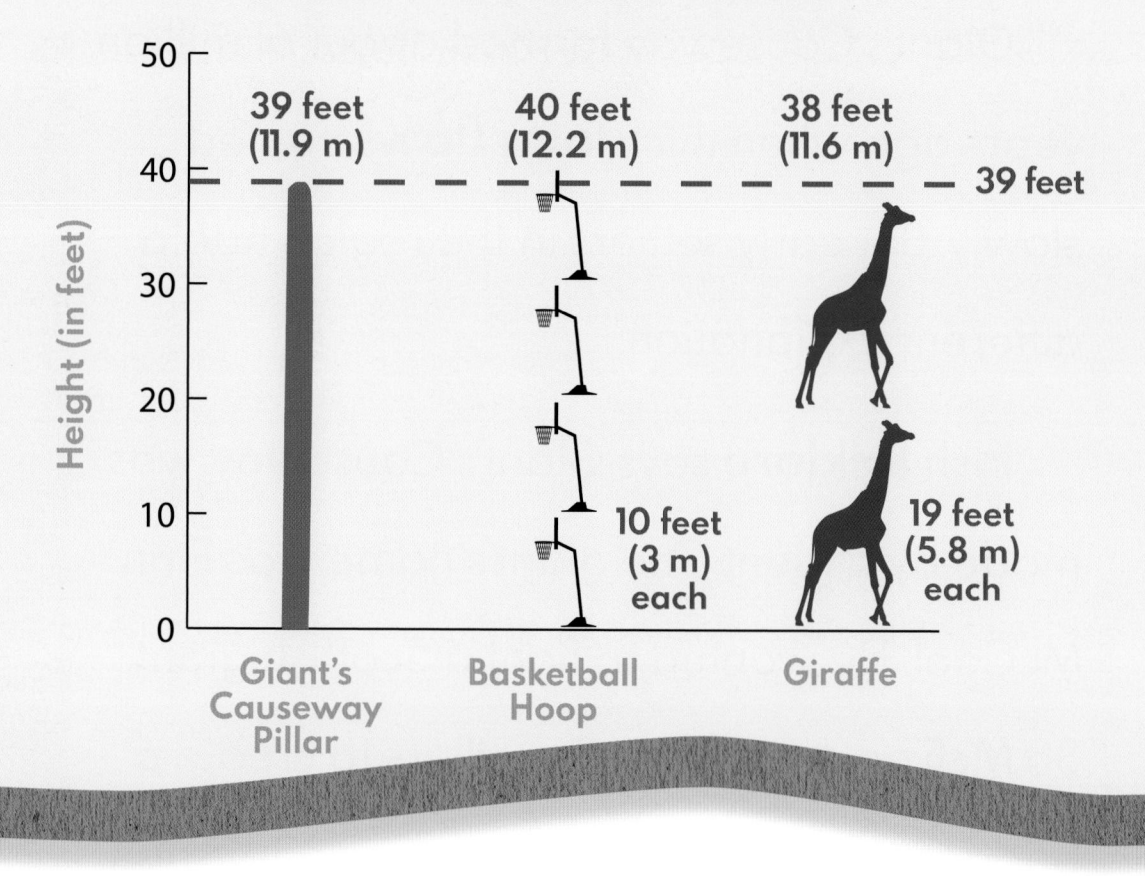

The tallest pillars at Giant's Causeway are about the height of four basketball hoops or two giraffes.

has 40,000 exposed stone columns. Some are short. Visitors can walk on these stones. Others are up to 39 feet (11.9 m) tall. There are many more columns hidden under the ocean and under Northern Ireland's grassy pastures.

Giant's Causeway formed about 61 million years ago when thick **lava flows** cooled slowly. But early settlers in the region had a different explanation.

Irish **folklore** says Giant's Causeway was made by a giant. The giant's name was Finn McCool. He wanted to fight a Scottish giant. So McCool laid down the pillars to create a bridge to Scotland. Then he fell asleep. The Scottish giant came across the bridge. McCool's wife told the Scottish giant that McCool was her baby. Afraid at how large the baby's father must be, the Scottish giant fled back home, destroying the bridge. The story says that the rocks are what remains of it.

There are many legends about Finn McCool, *right*, who is sometimes pictured with his wife.

Giant's Causeway is a fun place to visit for kids and adults alike.

Giant's Causeway covers 558 acres (226 ha). Many people visit Giant's Causeway each year. People learn how the columns formed. With so many visitors, it is important to protect Giant's Causeway. If people do not take care of it, the rocks can be damaged.

Explore Online

Visit the website below. Did you learn any new information about Giant's Causeway that wasn't in Chapter One?

Tall Stories: Were Giants Real?

abdocorelibrary.com/giants-causeway

Lava flows are very hot. They typically travel slowly across the ground.

CHAPTER 2

PERFECT STEPS

Millions of years ago, North America was attached to Europe. As they split apart, the Atlantic Ocean filled the gap. About 61 million years ago, deep cracks had formed in the land near Giant's Causeway.

The cracks released some of the largest volcanic eruptions ever known. Huge lava flows blanketed everything in sight.

Forming Columns

The **lava** cooled slowly. As it cooled, it formed a solid rock called basalt. As the basalt cooled more, it **contracted**, or shrank. Small cracks formed on the lava's surface. As the lava cooled, the cracks grew deeper and larger. The cracks

Basalt

Basalt is a type of volcanic rock. It is often dark in color. When it cools, the basalt sometimes forms a six-sided column. The width of the column depends on how fast the lava cools.

A shape with six sides is called a hexagon.

joined together at 120-degree angles to form

six-sided columns, or hexagons. Because not all

of the cracks joined exactly as they should, some

columns ended up with five or seven sides.

Waves are one of many forces that wear away at the columns.

Most of the columns are 15 to 20 inches (38–51 cm) wide. They used to all be about the same height. But over time, the columns began to **erode**. Ocean waves wore away pieces of basalt. Some of the columns broke.

Those columns washed away. Now some of the columns are very tall. Others are short. Near the shoreline, columns can be only a couple of feet tall.

Giant's Causeway continues to change. In recent years, tourists began to visit the site. Walking on the columns can make them wear down faster. It is important to protect the columns and the surrounding land.

Further Evidence

Look at the website below. Does it give any new evidence to support Chapter Two?

How Are Rocks Made?

abdocorelibrary.com/giants-causeway

The National Trust helps keep Giant's Causeway in its beautiful natural state.

CHAPTER 3

IN THE FUTURE

Giant's Causeway is part of a
protected area. It is a World
Heritage Site. The United
Kingdom's National Trust cares
for the property. Because it is a
World Heritage Site, laws protect
the land from human actions.

Sometimes local school groups visit Giant's Causeway.

A Popular Destination

More than 1 million people visit Giant's

Causeway each year. The National Trust saw

that more people were visiting every year. It worried that the columns might be damaged.

Before Giant's Causeway was a World Heritage Site, people took some of the rocks. People are no longer allowed to do that. However, people can still hurt Giant's Causeway in smaller ways. Human foot traffic can damage the columns.

Protected Home

Giant's Causeway is not just a beautiful place. It is also home to many kinds of plants and animals. More than 200 types of plants grow there. About 50 types of birds also live at Giant's Causeway.

Walking on the columns and cliffs speeds up erosion. People's shoes wear away tiny pieces of basalt. Wind and waves break apart the columns further. Over time, the columns may become unstable.

The National Trust does not want to stop erosion from happening. It is a normal part of any natural landscape. But the National Trust does want to prevent human-caused erosion. The trust still allows people to walk on the columns. Scientists monitor the area for damage. Then the trust can make rules to protect the area if needed.

In 2018, the National Trust began a study. The study looked at how people use the park. This would help the Trust decide how to change

Paths protect the columns from visitors' feet.

the paths. People use paths to get to different parts of the park. It is important that people do not leave the paths. This can hurt the plants and speed up erosion.

It is important to protect these stunning stone pillars for people to enjoy in the future.

Wider paths and more places to look out over the causeway will help the whole park. It will be more accessible to people. The trust works to make sure people can continue to enjoy Giant's Causeway for years to come.

Heather McLachlan is the director of the National Trust in Northern Ireland. She explained why Giant's Causeway is such an important site:

> *The Giant's Causeway offers visitors the opportunity to marvel at this area of outstanding beauty whilst unlocking the stories of the stunning rock formation.*

Source: "Giant Numbers with Causeway." *Belfast Telegraph*, 19 Dec. 2017, belfasttelegraph.co.uk. Accessed 17 Feb. 2019.

What's the Big Idea?

Read this quote carefully. What is its main idea? Explain how the main idea is supported by details.

MAP

GIANT'S CAUSEWAY

NORTHERN IRELAND

REPUBLIC OF IRELAND

ATLANTIC OCEAN

SCOTLAND

UNITED
KINGDOM

N
W E
S

ENGLAND

WALES

- Giant's Causeway formed 61 million years ago.

- The columns formed when basalt rock cooled, contracted, and cracked.

- Erosion has worn down some columns more than others.

Glossary

causeway
a raised strip of ground that runs across a body of water

contracted
became smaller as a result of cooling or drying out

erode
wear away by water, wind, or ice

folklore
a story about history that may not be entirely factual and that has been passed from generation to generation

lava
liquid rock from below Earth's surface that has reached the surface

lava flows
sheets of liquid or solid lava

Online Resources

To learn more about Giant's Causeway, visit our free resource websites below.

Visit **abdocorelibrary.com** or scan this QR code for free Common Core resources for teachers and students, including vetted activities, multimedia, and booklinks, for deeper subject comprehension.

Visit **abdobooklinks.com** or scan this QR code for free additional online weblinks for further learning. These links are routinely monitored and updated to provide the most current information available.

Learn More

Olson, Elsie. *Exploring the Rock Cycle: Petrologists at Work!* Abdo Publishing, 2018.

Petersen, Christine. *Discover Rocks.* Abdo Publishing, 2020.

Index

About the Author

Martha London writes books for young readers full-time. When she isn't writing, you can find her hiking in the woods.